A HARD ROAD TO TRAVEL

GOD'S PRESENCE AND MIRACLES IN MY LIFE

DR. DARRYL E. ALLEN

WWW.TRUEVINEPUBLISHING.ORG

A Hard Road To Travel
By Dr. Darryl E. Allen

Published by
True Vine Publishing Co.
810 Dominican Dr.
Nashville, TN 37228
www.TrueVinePublishing.org

Printed in the United States of America—First printing.

ACKNOWLEGDEMENTS

This book is dedicated to my beloved mother, who taught me how to love, made me proud of who I was, and introduced me to Christ.

To my father, who showed me the true value of a man and family.

To my loving wife, my true soulmate, who has stood by my side through it all.

To my children, into whom I have poured my heart and soul—who have shaped me into the man I am today and whom I am so proud of.

To my siblings, who have been my mentors and whom I have looked up to all my life.

And to all my family and friends from Harrisburg, Pennsylvania, who have given me so many great memories.

TABLE OF CONTENTS

INTRODUCTION

Like most middle-class Americans, my life has been a rollercoaster of many ups and downs. It's filled with cherished stories of childhood and family, tough teenage years, becoming an adult, marriage—and the struggles that come with trying to build a life with another person while still finding yourself—raising children, losing parents and siblings, and moving away from my hometown. Through it all, I've found that the ultimate goal in life is to submit to the will of God. Through God, we can truly find and understand our existence, strengthen our families, and accomplish things in life that we never thought possible.

Each of us has a journey that may seem unique to only us, but as we live, learn, and engage with others, we realize that our experiences are often very similar. Many never find God and spend their entire lives struggling with the burdens of the world and the evil it can bring. Job 14:1 says, "Man that is born of a woman is of few days and full of trouble."

My story is filled with memories of growing up in Harrisburg, PA, surrounded by family and friends, moving south, and facing the trials and tribulations that life brings. As I look back, I can see— as plain as the nose on my face— that God was always there, carrying me through it all and bringing me out on the other side a better man. I am forever thankful for His grace and mercy.

ESCAPING ADDICTIONS

"The only escape from a drug addiction is when the users mind comes into synch with the heart in wanting to quit. So long as the mind may believe it wants to quit, and the heart is still in love with those people, places, and things.... you can never stop."

The year was 1987, and the time was approximately 1 p.m. on a beautiful, sunny summer afternoon. I found myself driving down 14th Street in Harrisburg, PA, on my way to buy cocaine. As I passed the houses, I saw people sitting on their porches, enjoying the afternoon with their family and friends, and I began to cry like a baby. I wanted to do what they were doing. I didn't want to be out on the prowl for drugs. I wanted to feel normal again, to be at home with my family. But the addiction was strong, and as much as my mind didn't want to do what I was doing, I couldn't turn around. The addiction had my heart. I wiped the tears from my face and continued on my journey.

This journey, which had begun in the fall of 1986, led me to some very dark and dangerous places I never could have imagined. In the early 1980s, crack cocaine had been formally introduced to African American communities nationwide. It had started in California and quickly spread across the country. Between 1982 and 1985, the number of cocaine users had increased by 1.6 million people. I had been naïve to crack cocaine, though I had seen the effects of cocaine on intravenous addicts. I had no idea what was about to happen in my life. I had been smoking a little weed and drinking alcohol on occasion since I was 14, but what I was about to indulge in would take me through three years of a life I never could have imagined. The question was: how had I gotten there, and how would I get out?

This book was written as a testimony of my life and, hopefully, as an inspiration to others who may have been going through addictions or similar struggles. I hoped they would know that God had been with them and that they could change—but the change had to happen in the heart.

I

MY BEGINNING

It all started on May 19, 1960, at Harrisburg Hospital in Harrisburg, Pennsylvania. I was the last of six children born to Linwood and Bessie Allen, both forty years old at the time of my birth. I was born prematurely at seven months, weighing only one pound, and was kept in an incubator for two months before I was able to go home. My family told me how they would come to the hospital every day to visit me and always wanted to take me home with them.

After coming home, I developed a very weak respiratory system and was often sick. My mother told me that there were twenty-four viruses that year, and I caught every one of them. On one occasion, I developed a fever of over 106 degrees, turned blue, and went into convulsions. At that time, my sister Anita (who was seventeen) had a boyfriend in the armed forces who would call her collect, which led to our phone being turned off.

My mother told me that she handed me to one of her friends so that she could run to a neighbor's house to call my doctor. Her friend asked, "What if he dies?" and my mother answered, "Well, there's nothing you can do." To my mother's surprise, when she entered the neighbor's house, my doctor was already calling their phone.

By the time I was around four or five years old, I began to realize that I couldn't hear in my right ear. Later in life, I would learn that fevers over 106 degrees in children can cause nerve deafness in the ears, and I realized that's what had happened to me. This was the first time I recognized that God had saved me, but it wouldn't be the last time He saved my life.

FIRST MEMORIES

Growing up in Harrisburg, PA, was a very fun time. I was born on Cameron Street in an area that, at the time, was called Shipoke. I can remember some aspects of the house, but that's about all. My mom's father lived with us there, and his name was Tapley Gaines. He was an Indian from Chicago who had moved to Kentucky, Tennessee, and then to Steelton, PA.

My siblings called him "Pappa Daddy," and they told me many stories about him—how he used to play with them and taught my brothers how to fish and hunt. They all loved him. By the time I was born, he had grown old. My mom told me that I was getting most of the attention, and he used to step on my fingers because he was jealous. He told her that he would never live to hear me call his name. He died before I turned one year old, and he never did.

By the time I was two or three years old, I was talking like an adult. Since all my siblings were grown or nearly grown, I was always around them and picked up their way of speaking. Some say that by the time I was three, I was cussing like a sailor. I don't necessarily remember cursing that much, and if I did, I must have been sneaky because none of my family members ever heard me.

My sister Patsy took me almost everywhere she went. I remember her telling a story about one time when she was out walking me in a stroller and got into a fight with another girl. She said that I was in the stroller hollering,

"Get her, Patsy! Get her!" I don't remember this, but one of her friends later told me the same story, so it must have been true.

We moved from the house on Cameron Street in 1962 and lived across from what is now called Reservoir Park on Walnut Street. I remember looking out the window at night into the park across the street. It always seemed spooky, with a single light shining in the distance. My brother Tommy would tell me, "It's the Boogeyman! The Boogeyman is up there!" I was terrified whenever I looked in that direction.

I can still recall a day when I was about three years old, playing in the backyard on my swing. A dirty-looking Black man walked into the yard—the darkest-skinned person I had ever seen. I jumped off my swing and ran behind my sister Patsy, hollering, "The Boogeyman! The Boogeyman!" I'll never forget the way the man looked at me, as if I had lost my mind. My sister just laughed and said, "Darryl, that's the trash man, boy." I was so relieved, but it was their fault for making me believe a Boogeyman was hanging out in the park across the street in the first place.

When I was about four years old, I wandered down to the pet store on the corner of Eighteenth and Walnut Street. They had a boa constrictor in a cage, and the store owner pulled it out and put it around my neck. I was thrilled to have a snake around my neck that could have easily killed me. Proud of my bravery, I rushed home to tell my parents. My dad stormed down to the store, cussed the owner out, and I was never allowed back in there again.

On Christmas morning in 1963, I got my first tricycle

and rode it all day long. The next day, I could barely walk, and my mother and I were scheduled to fly to Kentucky to visit my great-aunt. My parents, along with my sister Patsy, rushed me to the emergency room at Harrisburg Hospital. The doctors ran all kinds of tests, and one came in and told them he thought I had developed polio. Then another doctor came in and asked if I had done anything unusual the day before. My sister quickly spoke up: "Yeah, he's been riding his tricycle all day." Thank God for that! They quickly determined that it wasn't polio—I was just having muscle spasms.

I also remember the day President John F. Kennedy was assassinated in 1963. I was three years old, and whenever he came on TV to address the nation, I would watch him like an adult, as if I understood everything he was saying. Even at that young age, I believed he was a good man working to improve the condition of African Americans in our country. It was a difficult time for Negroes (as we were called then), and his loss was deeply felt in our community.

During that time, I watched as Martin Luther King led marches, people were bitten by police dogs, and others were hosed down by the fire department. It was scary to witness as a child, and I believed the president was working to bring about change and put an end to the chaos. Then, on that day, I was riding my tricycle when the news came on the TV that the president had been assassinated. Everyone was devastated and crying, including me. I remember my mother looking at me in astonishment that I understood what had happened and was crying.

In the summer of 1964, I had a small pool set up in the backyard. One afternoon, I threw several of my toys into the pool before getting in, and one of them was a swinging monkey on a bar. It had a handle, and when I turned it, the monkey would swing around the bar. It was one of my favorite toys, even though it was broken. My mom kept telling me to get rid of it, but I couldn't bring myself to throw it away. Then, as I stepped into the pool, I stepped right on that monkey, and it cut a deep gash up the side of my ankle. I fell into the pool face-down, and my sister Patsy ran over and picked me up. They rushed me to the ER, where I received several stitches.

My brother Tommy had been the youngest for so long that when I came along and started getting all the attention, he became a little jealous. He would pick on me and try to get me into trouble. One day, I went into the bathroom to pee, and he was there too. Just as I was about to go, he told me to pee in the bathtub, which, being the mischievous three-year-old that I was, I did. As soon as I did, he hollered to our mother, "Mom, Darryl peed in the bathtub!" Well, Mom was smart enough to know that he was usually behind things like that, and he ended up getting in trouble instead of me.

Eventually, in 1965, we moved from that house to one on Seventeenth Street. It was only about a block from the old house and wasn't quite as big. Before we moved in, a policeman must have lived there because we found billy clubs and other weapons that the police used. In the early to mid-sixties, Black families began moving into the houses in our neighborhood, which we called "The Hill," and many white families started moving out. Many of them relocated across the river to what was called the "West Shore." Harrisburg was split into three main sections: The Hill, Southside, and Uptown.

Our house was located on the corner of Seventeenth Street and Apricot Street (an alley). On the other side of the alley was Lincoln Elementary School. At that time, Apricot Street had the school on one side and several small row homes on the other.

There were dirt alleys between and behind the row homes on Apricot Street and Elm Street, which was the next block over. I had many friends in the neighborhood, and we had a great time running through the little alleys between the homes. Directly behind the houses was the school's playground.

We had a small backyard with some grass, but Dad eventually had it paved with concrete to make it easier to clean up after the dog. Over time, they tore down all the houses in the alley and on Elm Street, turning the space into a huge parking lot for the teachers and residents who lived on that side of Seventeenth Street. Alongside the parking lot was the playground, which had swings, a basketball court, and a playground spinner. After school hours, it became a massive playground for all the neighborhood kids.

We had more football and baseball games on the playground than I could remember. There were lights that came on at night on the courts, and for a while, they held city league basketball games there. In the early to mid-seventies, they built basketball courts in Reservoir Park across from where we used to live, and they moved all the league games up there. However, we still had our court and our little neighborhood games on the playground. We even shoveled off the snow in the winter on the basketball court so we could play.

There were a lot of athletes in our neighborhood and city—many who went on to high school, college, and even the pros, especially in football. I was one of the fastest kids on the block at my age, and my brother Tommy taught me how to throw and catch a football. I remember some of the older guys in the neighborhood noticing how fast I was. They would ask me to run from one point to another and watch me in amazement, saying, "Wow."

In 1970, we got a puppy that we named "Mr. Bigg." He was a mix of German Shepherd and Collie that we adopted from the pound. He grew huge and would bark and growl at everyone who walked down the alley. A lot of people were scared of him and would go all the way around the block just to avoid passing by. Little did they know, he wouldn't bite anyone, but he was the best watchdog we ever had. In the winter, when it snowed, my friends and I would take him with us to the park to sled. I would tie my sled to his collar, and he would pull it up the hill before I sledded all the way back down.

We had some great times in that park, from sledding to playing tackle football. One day, we were playing tackle football, and I went out for a touchdown pass. I faked everyone out, and when I caught the ball, I looked up and ran straight into a tree. I busted my head and nose, and I think it may have knocked me out for a second or two. The guys picked me up and carried me across State Street (a four-lane major city street) to the fire station on the corner. The firemen checked me out and called my parents, who came and got me. They told them that I had a concussion and advised them to try to keep me awake for a while.

There was a Catholic church across the street from our house, and although we were in the hood, it remained an all-white church. Every Sunday, the churchgoers would park in the lot behind our house, get out of their cars, walk right past us on their way inside, and never speak. Then, in the early seventies, they installed bells on the church that rang every fifteen minutes—all day, every day. You could hear them throughout the whole neighborhood, and since we lived right across the street, it was especially loud. At first, it drove us crazy, and it was hard to sleep, but after a few years, we got so used to it that we didn't even notice it anymore.

My Mother

My mother was the love of my life. She was born in March 1921 in Madison, Kentucky. When I was born, my parents were forty years old, and all of my siblings—except for my brother Tommy, who was nine years older than me—were well into their teens or already grown with families. So, in many ways, I had my mom all to myself. My brothers and sisters always told me how bad I was growing up and how I got away with things they couldn't. I could do no wrong in my mom's eyes, and she gave me so much love.

As a kid, she spent a lot of time with me. She would take me to the park in the mornings, and we would play and roll in the grass. At night, she always read books and sang songs to me. She raised me to say prayers at mealtimes and bedtime. She introduced me to the Bible and told me that Jesus loved me, often singing the *Jesus Loves Me* song. I didn't know who Jesus was then, and all I saw in books was a white man with long blond hair and blue eyes. He certainly didn't look like anyone I knew, but since my mom had poured so much love into me, I felt that if He loved me, then I loved Him too.

She also sang a song every night titled *Anything You Can Do, I Can Do Better.* She sang that song to me until I believed it. As a result, I always felt confident in myself and excelled at almost everything I put effort into. It instilled a perfectionist streak in my personality.

When I was nine years old, my mother developed cancer in her larynx and had to undergo a laryngectomy. She was one of the first Black women to have the surgery, and on my tenth birthday, her procedure was scheduled at Temple University Hospital. I remember my sister Patsy throwing a birthday party for me that day to try and cheer me up. Though it helped a little, I was still depressed, not knowing whether my mom was going to live or die.

After the surgery, when we were finally able to see her, I remember walking into her room and seeing her head swollen to three times its actual size. She was almost unrecognizable. It was a shock, but it didn't matter to me—

my mother was alive. I was so happy to see her that when it was time to go, my dad had to carry me out of the room crying because I didn't want to leave.

During her time in the hospital, my dad and I really bonded. I remember a TV show that was on back then called *The Courtship of Eddie's Father,* starring Bill Bixby. It was about a father raising his son, and it reminded me of the life my dad and I were living during that time without my mom. I watched it every day. We spent a lot of time in Philly visiting my mom and staying with relatives.

During our stays in Philly, I played football with the kids in the neighborhood, and each time, they argued over whose team I was on. One time, when we were staying in North Philly with a man who was my dad's cousin, the boys gathered around me. I thought they were going to pick teams, but instead, they told me that if I didn't join their gang, I'd better not come around there again. When I told my dad, it was the last time we stayed there.

After a month or two in the hospital, she came home, and for a while, she couldn't talk. I would talk to her, and she would write me notes. Then I began to learn to read her lips—she could just move her lips, and I would know exactly what she was saying. She began to improve and get stronger every day, and then one day, she spoke.

She was on the front porch one afternoon while my sister was talking about something, and suddenly, she said, "Shiiiit!" We all laughed in amazement—not just because she had spoken, but because of all things, that was the first word to come out of her mouth.

Soon, she began speaking in sentences and then full paragraphs. Many people who undergo that surgery still rely on microphones or other devices to amplify their voice, but my mom could speak without any of that. In order to talk, she had to learn to use her diaphragm to create a belch and turn it into words. To someone listening, she might have sounded like she had a bad cold, but you could understand every word she said. It was amazing, and to this day, I have only ever heard one other person speak the way she did.

She went on to give lectures at universities and on public television about the negative effects of smoking. She also visited other patients who had undergone the same surgery, encouraging them to believe that, with effort, they too could learn to speak as she had. At that time, many people gave up and died because they didn't want to live that way.

I believe in my heart that it was nothing but God. He knew I needed my mother, and He gave her the strength and ability to come back and continue raising me as normally as possible. Everyone in the neighborhood seemed to know about her condition, and if I was out playing when the streetlights came on or it was time to eat, she couldn't shout for me—so she would come outside and clap her hands. All the kids in the neighborhood recognized her clap, and even if I was blocks away, they would run to get me and tell me my mom wanted me to come home.

She was able to return to work, and she retired at sixty-five. The following year, she became ill with a disease called dermatomyositis, which affects recovering cancer patients. It essentially breaks down the muscles and skin. She lived with the disease for ten years and passed away in March of 1997.

I was thirty-seven years old at the time of her passing. Though she had been sick for a decade and I had tried to prepare myself, her loss devastated me. I thank God for the time He gave me with her during the crucial years of my life when I needed her most.

It took me six years before I could talk about her and remember the good times we had without breaking down in tears. During those years, I tried to forget her as my way of coping with the grief. Then God sent me three dreams of my mother. In the third dream, she was at a playground, running and playing with a lot of other children. She came to me and said, "I just wanted you to know that I am okay and that I will not be coming to you again."

I have never had another dream about my mother. I know it was nothing but God because it was the closure I needed to move on. Today, I never say that she died—I only say that she has passed.

MY FATHER

My dad was born in January 1921 to Henry Allen, born in July 1890, and Bessie Garnett, born in February 1902. Both were from Bowling Green, Virginia. My grandfather Henry was the firstborn of 18 children to Lewis Washington and Louisa Allen. Lewis was from the Washington plantation, owned by John Washington, the nephew of George Washington. John Washington was a Confederate officer who was killed in an ambush in 1861 during a reconnaissance mission at the Battle of Cheat Mountain in West Virginia.

Louisa Washington-Allen was from the plantation of William Allen. Henry was born out of wedlock and kept his mother's maiden name, Allen. It was said that he had issues with his father and that his siblings tried to convince him to change his last name to Washington, but he never did.

The names of the other seventeen siblings were Luther, Clara, Frank, Willie, John, Sallie, Lizzie, George, Acc, Jennie, Tommie, Annie, Cary, Herbert, Clarence, Elwood, and Other. "Other" was born in 1894, and apparently, they ran out of names, so they named him "Other."

Eventually, Louisa Washington left my grandfather, Lewis Washington, and moved to Connecticut, where she became one of the first formerly enslaved women to marry her former slave owner, Dr. Tolliver. Together, they had six more children, bringing the total number of her children to twenty-four.

Today, most of the Washington family can be found in Virginia, Maryland, and the Washington, D.C. area. If you know anyone from these areas with the last name Washington, there's a good chance they are my relative.

My grandparents' move to Steelton, Pennsylvania, was not under good circumstances. Supposedly, my grandmother was raped by her uncle, and shortly afterward, my grandfather went to Steelton, got a job in the steel mill, and found a home. He then went back and brought my grandmother to live with him. This rape resulted in the birth of my uncle George Allen, a fact that remained a secret for a long time. He looked nothing like his other siblings, and as the old saying goes, "What's done in the dark will eventually come to light."

My grandparents had six children altogether: George, Linwood, Willie, Annie Mae, Charles, and Robert. Willie was born in 1923 and died at the age of five or six from pneumonia.

By the time I was born, my grandparents were already up in age and had moved just a few blocks from our house on Seventeenth Street. After Uncle George returned from the war, he lived with them in that house long after they had passed, staying there until he died in 1999.

Uncle George was a World War II veteran who went missing in action in Italy for a period of time and was believed to have been killed in battle. However, after several years of being missing, he showed up alive—apparently, he had found himself a woman and had been shacked up with her the whole time.

I remember visiting my grandparents' house and always sneaking into Uncle George's room to look at his collection of adult magazines.

When we visited my grandparents, we would sit around the table while Uncle George told ghost stories that scared me to death. He would always give me money to run down to the corner store to buy him some cigars, and I could always keep the change.

My grandfather was a very quiet man. He always sat in his little chair in the dining room, right next to the eat-in kitchen. He only ever said four words to me that I can remember, and that was when I went to touch anything in the dining room. He would be sitting there, looking as if he were asleep, and when I reached out to touch something, he would look up at me and say, "Don't touch that, boy."

At first, it used to scare me, but then I started doing it on purpose just to mess with him—just so he would say it.

Strangely enough, they never visited us, and later I found out it was because they didn't like my mom. We never received any gifts or anything from them. I would see them occasionally when they pulled their old Buick out of the garage to go to church; they would drive right past our house—sometimes even on the wrong side of the street. Fortunately, there weren't as many cars on the road back then as there are today.

Growing up, we never knew any of our Washington relatives. The only relative I ever knew was my Aunt Dolly Tolliver and her family, who lived in Washington, D.C. We visited her quite often, along with her daughters and their families, who lived just outside of D.C. in Maryland. Aunt Dolly was one of the daughters of the Tolliver family in Connecticut, descended from my great-grandmother Lousia Washington.

We became the lost tribe of the Washington family in Harrisburg, Pennsylvania, carrying the name Allen. As far as the Allens were concerned, my dad's brothers— Uncle Charles had four children, and Uncle Robert (Mex) had three children—while my parents had six of us who bore the Allen name. I must admit that, over the years, I contemplated changing my last name to Washington. But with my kids already carrying the Allen name, it would have caused too much confusion. Besides, the thought of changing my name to another slave master's name wasn't appealing, so I decided to leave it alone. In the early 2000s, I met a cousin from the Washington family, and we still keep in touch today.

My earliest memories of my dad are filled with him drinking, arguing, and fighting with my mom. He used to beat my mother in the years before I was born, though I don't remember much of that as a child. However, I do recall two incidents where he hit her. Once, when I was around four years old, he came home drunk and broke a plate in her face while she was asleep. I cried when I saw her face the next day. The next time was around Christmas, and I was no older than five. I came down the steps while they were arguing, and I saw him slap her. I got between them and told him to stop, but he pushed me out of the way, saying, "Get the hell out of here!" I remember thinking to myself, *I'm gonna kill that motherfucker when I get older.*

I heard that my brother Linwood once told him, while he was in high school, that if he ever put his hands on our mom again, he would kill him. After my mother's surgery, the abuse stopped altogether. As the years passed and Mom got sick, he had to care for her. She remembered all the beatings and resented him so much that she once said she hated him. Before she passed, she told me she was spending every dime she had so he would get nothing—and she pretty much did.

We would always sit around the dining room table, drinking, and then he'd start talking about how he used to beat up guys and what he'd do—or had done—to a "nigga." He hated white folks and dark-skinned Black people, and I could never figure out why, considering he was brown-skinned himself. He would say that he never knew a dark Black man who was worth a nickel, yet he had dark-skinned friends.

He loved his cars, and the only time I ever saw him cry was when someone crashed into his Buick and totaled it. He cried like a baby, and I laughed. One day, my little niece and I were in the car with him, driving up State Street, when a drunken white guy rear-ended us at a stoplight. My dad got out and beat the crap out of that man.

On another occasion, we had been at the house drinking and talking as we normally did on weekends when a guy walked down the alley beside our house, firing a .22-caliber pistol into the school building next door. We all ducked down until he passed. When we finally got up and went outside to see the damage, my dad noticed the guy had put a few bullet holes in his car—and he took off after him.

Dad must have been in his sixties and had recently had knee surgery, while I was in my mid-twenties. I took off trying to catch him, but by the time I caught up, he had already wrestled the gun out of the guy's hand, pinned him to the ground, and had his hand in his back pocket, about to cut him with the pocketknife he always carried. I was amazed at how fast he could run with a bad knee. That was the moment I realized where my siblings and I got our speed from.

Dad became a Mason in his later years, and I thought that was an impressive accomplishment for a man with only a seventh-grade education. One day, when he was seventy-five years old, he looked lonely and said, "All of my friends are gone." That has always haunted me, making me wonder if I could end up like that someday.

At the end of the day, my dad taught me the importance of family and responsibility. He would always say, "I'll sleep in the basement before I let another man come up in here and raise my kids." Words that I learned to live by.

MY SIBLINGS

My siblings were much older than me. My brother Peewee (Linwood Carter) was the oldest, followed by my sister Anita Hill. Next came my brother Linwood Allen Jr., then William (Billy), Patricia (Patsy), and Thomas (Tommy). Tommy was nine years older than me and three years younger than Patsy, who was three years younger than Billy, who was three years younger than Linwood, who was also three years younger than Peewee. My dad also had a son in Philadelphia named Jimmy.

For my fifty-second birthday, my brother Tommy wrote me a letter describing what he called "The Power of Three," which highlighted each sibling:

My youngest brother enjoyed his 52nd birthday in 2012. As a result, I wanted to give him something unique and special for his day. As I began writing, I realized that I was blessed enough to have a unique experience with all my siblings. Therefore, I have decided to share my feelings to honor my love for the people I grew up with and how they positively affected my life.

The first son was born in a magical year that began the "Power of the Three Legacies." The theory behind the Power of Three is the ability to track each sibling's age based on a pattern in their birth years. A child in our family was born in one of three ways:

1. Every three years.
2. Each consecutive year for three years.
3. As an exponent of three squared (9).

Knowing these rules, you can determine the age of all your siblings simply by knowing your own age.

In 1940, the first was born. He was the "King of Laughter" and always the life of the party. Everyone in his presence felt like family. The gift of making someone laugh is the soul of mankind. We all enjoy laughter, but only a few have the ability to affect others in this most positive way. *(Peewee, 1940)*

Three years later, a beautiful daughter with gorgeous reddish skin tones was conceived. Her outer beauty was the initial attraction, but her inner strength developed values of trust, respect, and the highest level of character. Thus, this has become her legacy. *(Anita, 1943)*

Three years later, the first of three miracles appeared, born in three consecutive years. The first was a marvelous athlete who would not be denied his right to be born. Later in life, he utilized this *can't-stop-me* attitude to showcase athletic skills that are still talked about, even after his homecoming.

(Butch, 1946)

A year later, the most unique of the Power of Three was born and titled himself *"Born to Love."* An individual with unique thoughts and carefree ways, he secretly appeared on the scene to do things *his* way. To know yourself at an early age in life is the most powerful tool one can have. *(Billy, 1947)*

He was immediately followed by the arrival of the sweetest and most gorgeous bundle, with a blend of dark satin hair and the most perfect almond-colored skin. Initially thought to be the consummate *tomboy*, her legacy proved to be much deeper. She became the consummate mother figure—when Mom was working, she took care of her younger brother, ensuring his early protection and making sure he was fed. Today, she still seeks to obtain the highest level of being *a wonderful mother* to her two children. *(Patsy, 1948)*

Three years later, a little darker and a little heavier, with a superlative curiosity, the next child was born. He arrived with an innate desire to explore and see the world. Though welcomed immediately, he was also surrounded by a family mystery. After living in ten cities and six states, today, questions still arise about whether he has finally settled down once and for all. *(Tommy, 1951)*

Finally, the youngest was born with the awesome power of three squared (9). The late addition to the family opened his eyes to the world, armed with a sprinkling of all his siblings' attributes. His strengths equated to an innate ability to find a way where there is no way in all facets of life. Thus, he must be the power and envy of *all* the Three's.

(Darryl, 1960)

To all my siblings: Please understand that this is the internal love and vision that I profess for each of you. I am sure you have your own thoughts about how we projected ourselves during all the years we have been together. However, I hope you find this interesting and enjoy reading it as much as I have enjoyed reflecting on these wonderful life experiences I have had with each of you.

In loving memory of my brother Thomas "Tommy" Allen (1951–2021).

My sister Patsy was always there with me and for me. She got married at our house on 17th Street when I was seven or eight years old. I remember the pastor was a man who stuttered really badly. One of my friends and I were on the steps watching the ceremony, and when he started stuttering, we fell out laughing. They all made us leave. Patsy and her husband lived with us for a short time until she eventually moved. They relocated across town, and when I was ten, she had a baby girl. It was the first time I held a baby, and I immediately fell in love with her.

Patsy had a poodle puppy that she gave to us, and I named him Buffy. Buffy was around six months old when she gave him to us. At that time, there was a guy in the neighborhood who was a professional dog trainer, and he taught me how to train dogs. I trained Buffy so well that you didn't even need a leash to walk him. He was my dog, and he didn't care too much for anyone else. I was the only one who could pick him up without him growling.

Buffy was extremely smart. He would sit by my dad's

chair after he got a little older and let out gas. My dad would holler and say, "Take your ass up the stairs." Buffy would very reluctantly go up the stairs and look back at my dad as if to say, *"You son of a bitch."*

My sister Patsy returned to Harrisburg and bought a home just two doors down from ours. I was so happy to have her back. Buffy had long been housebroken, but every time I took him over to her house, he would cock his leg up and pee on her couch. He never did it anywhere else I took him—only at her house. I guess that was his way of paying her back for getting rid of him.

Eventually, Buffy got old and began to have seizures. One day, I came to visit my parents, and Buffy was gone. They told me they had to have him euthanized, and that really hurt me.

Today, Patsy and I are still very close. Though we live in separate states and don't see each other very often, we try to talk as much as we can.

My sister Anita got married when I was around three, and when I was five years old, she had a daughter who became like a little sister to me. She eventually divorced her husband and fell in love with a man twice her age. In 1972, they moved to Ohio. I was twelve years old and would go visit her during the summers. That first summer, I made friends quickly and had a lot of fun. I played football with the guys, and they all thought I was some kind of superstar.

The summer of 1974, just before going down there, some friends decided to steal a school bus, and I went along with their plan. We snuck onto the lot where the buses were parked, but when we got on the bus, there were no keys. One of the guys started messing around with the gears and took it out of gear, shifting it into neutral. The bus started drifting down the hill, and we all jumped out and ran.

Later, I heard on the news that it had rolled down into a home trailer. It caused a lot of damage and was under investigation. I had never been so happy to leave and go to Ohio as I was that summer.

That was my last summer going down there. By the time I was fifteen, I was playing organized football and had other interests, as teenagers do. But we always stayed in touch, and they came home to visit pretty often. She passed from a stroke in December 2024.

My brother Linwood "Butch" was a high school football star. He should have been drafted to the "Big 33" (a football game comprised of the best players from around the state of Pennsylvania); however, in the early 1960s, when he graduated, they weren't accepting Black players in that game. He taught me how to fish, and he and I would go fishing quite often. I learned to hook bait, scale, and gut fish at a very early age. He got married, had three beautiful daughters, and started working out of town, so we didn't get much time to fish after that.

He also loved to hunt. He would often catch rabbits and squirrels and give them to my dad to cook. Dad would clean them, skin them, and cook them in gravy with onions, carrots, and celery, which we would eat with biscuits. I used to love it. Once, he shot a deer and brought it home to clean in his basement. I can remember when the bowels came out—it was the worst smell ever, all through his house.

We always remained close, and he was always there for me if I needed anything. He passed from prostate cancer in 2009.

My brother William "Billy" Allen was born on May 18th. Ironically, my birthday is May 19th, though he was thirteen years older than me. My mother told me that she gave me to him when I was born as a birthday gift, and he was always there for me. He taught me to tie my shoes, how to drive, and so many other things. He spent a lot of time with me until, when I was around eight years old, he got into trouble and went to jail for five years.

We would visit him, and I can still remember going into the jail, seeing and hearing those bars open and close—it was very scary. I made up my mind then that I never wanted to be in a place like that, and by the grace of God, I never have been.

Billy was always my go-to sibling. Once he got out of jail, he never went back, but he was a really crazy guy. By that time, he was in his second marriage, and he would stay away from home for days at a time, out with other women. I asked him why he stayed away so much. He said, "If I go for two hours, I have to answer questions and go through a bunch of bullshit, and if I stay two days, I go through the same shit—so I might as well stay two days." Apparently, that didn't work so well, as they eventually divorced, and he moved to Philadelphia, where he passed in 2016 from prostate cancer.

My brother Thomas "Tommy" Allen was my coach and

mentor. He was a great high school football player, and he and I would throw the football all the time. I was really fast and could catch the football. He would put me up against some of his college friends who were defensive backs to try and cover me on pass plays. He would draw up a play for me, and I would go out, make a move on them, and catch the ball for touchdown passes over them all the time. They could never stop me, and he would fall out laughing at them.

He graduated from high school and went to college, where he had an outstanding college career. The Dallas Cowboys showed interest in him during his senior year, but during practice, he fell and dislocated his shoulder. He was out for most of his senior year and lost the opportunity to go pro. He graduated and went on to obtain his master's degree. We were all so proud of him because he was the only one in the family at that time who went to college and truly made something of himself.

He would always come home from college during my middle school and high school years, take me into a room, and lecture me about my behavior and bad grades. I would listen, but it all seemed to go in one ear and out the other. Though I respected him, he was still my brother, and I didn't feel like I had to listen to him. But he was the only one who at least acted as if they cared about what I was doing.

Today, I realize I wish I had listened to him—it would have made my life much easier and more productive. He never moved back home. He got married, had children, and eventually wound up in Atlanta, GA, before moving to

Nashville, TN, where he passed away from cancer in 2021.

Before my dad married my mom, he had two sons, Peewee and Jimmy. Jimmy lived in Philly, and according to the stories I've heard, no one knew about him until he popped up one day in the early sixties and announced to the family that he was my dad's son. He would always come with a gang of guys, and they said he was actually the leader of the gang.

When he came the first time, I heard that he had actually planned to kill my dad, but when he got there and met my family, he changed his mind. He was married and had four children. He and I didn't really get close until I was grown and able to drive to Philly to visit him. He was a Muslim most of his life and became a member of the Fruits of Islam (FOI). He passed in 1997 from intestinal cancer.

One of Jimmy's sons came to live with us for a while to get away from some trouble he had gotten into in Philly. He and I became very close, and one day, we decided we were going to become blood brothers. We got a needle and intended to prick our fingers to draw blood so we could press them together. It took us a long time because we were scared of the pain, but we finally did it and officially became blood brothers. Today, he and I are still very close. I call him my little brother, and he calls me big brother, though he is only a few years younger than me. I love him like he is my real brother.

My dad's other son, Linwood, who we called "Peewee," was an alcoholic for as long as I knew him. He would visit quite often, and I would sit on his lap and play with his beard until he got drunk and passed out, as he usually did. He had a family before I was born and kids my age or older. His kids were like brothers and sisters to me. They would come and spend the night, and we had a lot of fun sleeping in my bunk bed.

Peewee was the most hilarious person you would ever meet. He had all kinds of sayings that were so funny. For instance, if he didn't like you, he would say, "Mother made you, mother raised you, and mother fuck you." If he saw a woman with a big booty, he would look and say, "Good googa moo." Since my earliest memories of him, he never had any teeth. His gums were so hard that he could bite apples and crunch them up in his mouth better than some people with teeth. I asked him one day what happened to his teeth, and he replied, "I had a toothache so bad, I went to the dentist and told him to pull all them motherfuckers out."

His wife eventually left him, took all the kids, and moved to New York. I never really saw most of them again until the oldest son moved back to Harrisburg to finish high school there. I was so happy to see him, and he and I became close. He is five years older than me, and I remember telling him that he needed to call me Uncle. He said, "I ain't ever calling you Uncle." Today, he and I are really close, and he calls me Unc, and I call him nephew.

Peewee eventually remarried a white lady and had a beautiful daughter. I would go to visit them sometimes. We never really ate at their house because it wasn't very clean, and on one occasion, Billy and I went to visit on Thanksgiving

Day. Peewee's wife had cooked some chitterlings, and Peewee was slopping them up. She asked us if we wanted some, and we asked her how she had cleaned them. She replied, "Clean them?" with a confused look on her face. Billy and I looked at each other and said, "No, thank you." When we left, we laughed all the way back home because we knew white people don't know how to clean chitterlings, and Peewee was eating them like they were delicious. Peewee passed at the old age of eighty-two in 2023.

Today, I miss having my siblings around. They were always my inspiration to be successful in life. They had families, homes, nice cars, and blessed lives. I knew that when I grew up, I wanted to have those things in my life, and through the years of watching their growth and success, it made me want all the more to be successful too. I would remember the song my mother used to sing to me constantly as a child called, "Anything you can do, I can do better."

SCHOOL YEARS

Living across the alley from my elementary school, it only took me a few steps from my backyard into the school. My mother always kept a good rapport with my teachers, and it kept me from getting into trouble. I still have friends that I made in kindergarten, and one guy in particular, we have been best friends since then. During my elementary years, my mom would always buy me nice clothes. Being a light-skinned, curly-haired, well-dressed boy in the hood can be quite difficult. I spent several years getting bullied by a few boys, hiding and running home after school to avoid a fight.

Soon, desegregation began in our school district, and they bused me to a school that was a few miles away from our home. That was when I decided it was time to fight back. My first fight was in the fourth grade, with a kid who had been bullying me all year. I decided that I was tired of it, and this was the day. I stood up to fight, and this kid hit me so hard in the face, it spun me around 360 degrees. I got myself together and went at him, wrestled him into a corner, and was throwing punch after punch at him. I don't think I hurt him much, but it was enough to let him know that I wasn't taking any more of his crap.

The teacher was even tired of him bullying me because I remember the look on her face when they broke us up. She had a look as if she was so proud of me. He and I became best friends after that, and he never tried to fight or bully me again. We stay in contact even today. The next fight would be one to remember.

By this time, I was in the fifth grade, and my dad had somehow known of me getting bullied and began giving me fighting lessons. He was five feet, six inches tall and fought like Joe Frazier, with his hands covering his face and head, bobbing and weaving. At that time, Muhammad Ali was the champion, and I remember telling him that "I can't fight like that, Dad, I'm too small." I wanted to move and jab like Ali. That's when he told me that there were only three animals in this world that won't bite you when their backs are up against a wall. He asked if I knew what they were, and I replied "no." He said, "It's a sheep, a rabbit, and a coward." Then he asked me, "Which one are you?" I said, "Neither," and then he responded that fighting isn't fair and that I had weapons at my disposal, such as nails, teeth, feet, and even to grab a brick or a stick to use.

A few days after this, I came to school, and this kid was looking at me with a look like he was going to kill me. I asked a friend who was sitting next to me what was wrong with him. He replied, "He heard what you said about him." Apparently, someone told him that I had said something about him, and to this day, I don't know what I said or if someone lied on me. I have always been a jokester, and he had a bald head that I might have cracked a joke about; however, to this day, I don't really remember. The kid was way bigger than me, and he was always acting crazy, like he knew karate. I looked back at him again, and I was terrified.

In those days, when you wanted to fight, we would wait until it was time to use the restroom, and that's where the fights would take place, unless you could wait until after school. So, restroom time came, and I'm still sitting in my seat. All the guys said, "Darryl, you gotta go!" I got up and walked slowly into the restroom, and as soon as I got in there, he started making crazy sounds and throwing crazy swings and punches. I was ducking for my life as his fists were missing me and hitting the walls, and it sounded like he was cracking the walls.

I continued to duck and back up. Eventually, my back went up against the wall, and he grabbed me around my back in a bear hug, attempting to throw me on the floor. At that very moment, I could see my dad's face as plain as day, telling me about my fighting weapons. I looked down and saw nothing but his neck, and I bit that boy like Count Dracula. He started to scream and fell to his knees. I fell to my knees right with him, still with a pit bull lock on his neck, making growling noises.

He began hollering to all his boys, "Get him off, get him off!" That's when I bit down harder, started making louder growling sounds, and looked up at them. The boys got scared and all ran out, saying, "We don't have anything to do with it!" Soon, the teacher came in and pulled me off of him. A little later, I remember seeing him on the other side of the cafeteria, and I showed him my teeth again and growled. Needless to say, he never bothered me again.

The following year, in the sixth grade, there was another kid. He was a kind of fat kid and much bigger than my skinny little self. He was always picking on me and cracking jokes. It went on for most of the year without me doing anything, and somehow my dad found out about it. One sunny spring afternoon, he told me to take a ride with him. We never hung out much, and I was pretty excited to go, so I got in the car, and he pulled around the corner and parked in front of the kid's house. I asked him, "What are you doing?" and he said, "Get out the car!"

Now, I was really scared because this was the last thing I expected. He knocked on the door, and the kid's dad answered. His dad was over six feet tall, and my dad was much shorter. I was surprised to see they knew each other. They greeted each other, shook hands, and he asked us to come in. I walked in with my head down as this kid was staring at me hard. They had a short conversation, and during that time, this kid was still looking at me hard, and I continued to have my head down, trying not to look up.

Then suddenly, my dad said to the man, "Do you know your boy has been messing with my son for a while now, and I've had enough of it? So, the next time he messes with my son, I'm gonna kick your ass!" That's when I looked up in amazement and thought, What did he just say? All these years, he's been telling these gangster stories that I didn't believe, and now I believe he was really a gangster! The man attempted to reply, "I see my son's a little bigger than yours," and that's when my dad interrupted him and said, "Did you hear what I said? The next time that little fat bastard messes with my son, I'm gonna kick your ass." They stood up, shook hands, and we walked out. I remember walking in with my head down and walking out with my chest in the air, looking at the boy with a big smile on my face as I bopped out.

Eventually, I had to fight the kid. I sucker-punched him while getting off the bus and beat him up for making jokes about my mom. After that, I never had another problem with him. I learned that my dad had told me the truth—that fighting is not fair—and when it comes to bullies, all you have to do is fight back. It doesn't matter whether you win or lose; you just have to fight back, and they will never bully you again.

Life began to change for me during my seventh-grade year when I met one of my best friends to this day. He was one of the biggest guys in our class, and we connected on the first day of school that year. Going into seventh grade, I was a midget football quarterback for a team called the Packers, but I had never really played basketball before.

Since my new friend was the captain of our intramural team, he gave me a starting position as a guard. I was the worst basketball player on the team. We made it to the championship game, and in the last few seconds, somehow, the ball landed in my hands. I decided to take the final shot. Well, the ball went way over the basket and out of bounds. My friend grabbed me by the neck and wanted to kill me.

I continued playing midget football for the Packers during eighth grade, which was my final year with the team. That year, I started as quarterback, and we went undefeated, winning the championship game. I was a superstar that season, passing and running for several touchdowns every game. But none of my family came to see me play—except for one time when my brother Tommy came home and watched me. I was so excited to have him there. I remember running a touchdown, looking up into the stands at him, and seeing him and his friend giving each other a high five. That felt so good, and I was so proud. I ran five touchdowns that day.

For me, it was a kind of sad time because all of my other siblings were grown and gone, and I was left by myself with my parents. It felt as though I was an only child, with no one to turn to other than my friends. By ninth grade, I started hanging out with some guys in the neighborhood who were a few years older than me, and I began drinking and smoking weed. My grades dropped from A's to C's, and it seemed as though no one cared. My dad certainly didn't. He had only a seventh-grade education, and after raising his other kids and being in his mid-fifties at the time, it seemed that all he wanted for me was to finish school and leave.

I was still seriously into football and track, but the guys I was hanging out with were a bad influence on me. They were not only older but also larger in body frame, and they could always consume more alcohol than I could. I would try to keep up with them and would always end up throwing up by the end of the night.

One Saturday afternoon, when I was fourteen, I had a few dollars in my pocket and decided to go to the movies, but I couldn't find a girl to go with, so I went by myself. Before going, I bought a nickel bag of weed, rolled it all up into joints, and placed them in a plastic sandwich bag. I went downtown to the Colonial Theatre to see *Foxy Brown*, starring Pam Grier.

When you entered the theater, the front was all glass, with a glass door on each side. As you walked in, you went up an incline to a flat level where the concession stand was on the right-hand side. At that point, you could either go down into the seating area or down the steps to the restrooms. Guys were always in the restroom smoking weed before the movie started, and I decided that's what I would do that day.

I went down the steps into the restroom and lit my joint. I was enjoying it until a white guy came in, looked at me, and immediately turned around and walked back out. I knew he was going to tell on me. So, I took one last hit off the joint and put it down the sink. Then I went back to the toilet, thinking about flushing my bag of joints, but I changed my mind. I said, "Fuck that white boy," to myself. I walked up the stairs and could hear him saying that I was down there smoking weed.

I immediately said, "Exit, stage right," and started running out of the theatre. As I was running down the incline toward the door, I suddenly realized that I was not at the door. As I tried to stop, I noticed the white guy was chasing me. He came up behind me, gave me a push, and sent me crashing right through the glass front window. As I went through the glass, I turned and grabbed his tie, pulling his nose straight into a large shard of glass. The glass nearly ripped his nose off, leaving it dangling from his face.

Now, I found myself outside the theatre and in a daze, but before I could pull myself together, the guy started screaming. As I got to my feet, he grabbed my arm and threw a judo flip on me, sending my feet into the air before I landed hard on my back. He got on top of me, still screaming, with blood running everywhere as he tried to hit me. I had my hands up, blocking his punches, until two Black guys walking up the street saw what was happening. He looked up at them, and they looked at him and said, "You better get off of him right now." Somehow, I came through that with only a few minor scratches, and they took me home.

I told my parents the story, but of course, I told them that some other guys had been smoking down there, not me. They filed charges against the guy, who was about twenty-five years old. When it came time for court, we were informed that he was AWOL from the Navy and had been sent to jail. He was a grown man and had no business putting his hands on a fourteen-year-old kid. Today, when I think about it, I bet every time he looks in the mirror and sees the scar on his face, he thinks of me.

During ninth and tenth grade, I also ran track. I won all of my races in the one-hundred-yard dash and had a bunch of blue first-place ribbons. But, just like with football, no one came to see me. I kept running and playing football, but I was losing motivation while still smoking and drinking with my older friends. My grades continued to plummet to C's and D's. My mom couldn't control me, my dad didn't seem to care, and all my siblings were gone. I was home by myself, doing me.

During the summer, going into tenth grade I had a friend, whose mom worked at the vital statistics department at the state, and I talked her into making me a fake birth certificate so I could get a job and my license early. She did and I got a job working at a steak house called Ponderosa at fifteen years old, where I was hired as a grill cook, and learned how to cook steaks really good.

I loved the job, especially all the free meals I was getting, until one day they hired this white boy, and he thought he was better than me somehow. He kept trying to tell me what to do, and I told him that he was not my boss, and to leave me alone. He kept it up, and finally I told him "If you say one more thing, I gonna fuck you up". Then to be smart he literally said, "one more thing". I took a hot rack of potatoes and beat his ass. They fired me and walked me out. I was pissed, and said, "fuck all yall because I'll get another job".

One week later I got a job working at a produce distribution company. The owner was this big fat white guy that went to our church, and I asked him for a job as a delivery man, and he gave it to me. The first time I got in the truck I didn't even know how to drive a stick shift, and I remember bucking the truck all over the place, but I learned how to shift and drive it really quickly. I worked that job for most of that summer, and then there was a few complaints called in on me.

On one complaint, I went to deliver at a restaurant called the Alva, located at the train station downtown Harrisburg. It was six o'clock in the morning and there were several very large barrels of crackers used when serving soup. There were two crackers in each pack, and I was hungry so, I grabbed a few packs. I didn't think it would be a problem at all with so many. I wasn't trying to steal, as I took them right in front of everyone. Then, one of the chefs hollered out "Put those back". I was shocked and looked at the guy that was there showing me where to put the produce I was delivering, and he just shrugged his shoulders, as if to say there was nothing he could do so, I put them back.

When I got back to work, I was informed that they had called in and told my employer that I was trying to steal from their place of business and that they didn't want me back again. I was warned that if I made one more mistake,

I would be fired.

A week or so later, while making a delivery, I saw a guy I wanted to get some weed from. As I was turning the truck around at a gas station, the plywood covering the produce hit the top of the gas station sign and tore the whole thing off the truck. I was fired immediately.

One week later, I got another job with a different company doing the same kind of deliveries. On my first day, at six o'clock in the morning, I had just finished my first delivery downtown. As I was attempting to exit the alley onto Third Street to head to my next stop, a white guy was blocking the alley, letting his girlfriend off to work. He just sat there in his car as if I wasn't there, so I blew my horn for him to move. As the white girl got out, she passed my truck and called me a "nigger." I responded by calling her a "white bitch."

The guy heard me and, to be smart, backed up just a little—still not leaving me enough room to get out. So, I pulled up and very slightly bumped his bumper to be smart, but I caused no damage at all to either vehicle. We both got out. I was about to sucker punch him, but then I remembered it was my first day on the job. So, I got back in the truck and went about finishing my deliveries.

When I got back, my boss told me the guy had gone to the police station and reported that I hit him and ran. I was fired again.

By then, summer was almost over, but I had saved up enough money to buy a car. I found a 1969 Chevy Camaro. It was owned by a white guy who had modified it with all kinds of racing parts, and it was fast. The guy was selling it because he was going into the army, and I had to promise both him and my dad that I wouldn't race it.

It was a beautiful metallic blue with sport wheels, and the interior was super clean. I think I had the nicest car in the entire school going into my junior year. I was the starting varsity quarterback, and I had had the car for about a month when my dad had to have knee surgery.

On the first day of school, after seeing all the new sophomore girls, I decided I was going to quit the team and spend the year pulling girls instead. After football practice that day, I left my equipment on the floor with the intention of not returning. Instead of going to visit my dad at the hospital, I decided to go to the house of a girl I was trying to get at.

While sitting on the front porch of the girl's house, a guy pulled up in an old Ford Fairlane and challenged me to a race. I thought, "What the hell, I could use a few dollars." So, we went down to Cameron Street, slowed up traffic in front of a Dairy Queen, and took off racing.

In the first race, my gear got stuck in second, and I lost. So, I challenged him to double or nothing—knowing I didn't even have any money to cover the bet.

We raced again, and this time, I was about half a car length ahead of him. I was only in first gear, and I could hear that he was already in third. I knew that as soon as I hit second gear, it was over. I was looking over at him, laughing. Then, just as I shifted into second, my right front tire hit a ditch, and the entire front end lifted off the ground.

I lost control and ran the car into an empty lot, where an antique car was sitting on cinder blocks right next to the wall of a small house. My car went sideways, with the driver's side smashing into the old car, pushing it into the wall. The impact tossed my car into the air before it landed back on its wheels, now facing the street.

Luckily, I didn't get killed. I only needed a few stitches in my arm and had a busted nose from hitting the steering wheel.

Someone told me that about ten years before my accident, a guy named Charles Atwell had been driving the same path on a rainy day. He lost control of his car at the exact same spot and crashed into the wall of that house—only he was decapitated. I remember that my window was halfway down that day, and if that old car hadn't been there on those cinder blocks, I probably would have hit the wall the exact same way.

I went into a deep depression after that. I had worked hard all summer, gotten fired from every job, and now my car was gone. Then I heard that some of the neighborhood kids—who were always at my house checking out my car and bringing their cars over to clean—had been making jokes about the accident. The joke was that I had hit a boat on dry land. That wasn't true, but thinking back on it now, it's actually pretty funny.

I didn't go back to the football team afterward, and neither a family member nor a coach came to me to try and motivate me to return to the team or do anything positive with my life. Looking back, considering I was sixteen years old, the fastest on the team, and the quarterback, my life could have taken a different path if I had someone who showed interest in me—someone I could have talked to.

So, I finished that year without participating in anything. I just went to school, got high every day, and went home.

The summer of my junior year, going into my senior year, I got a job at a local daycare center doing administrative work, which included typing and filing. I was seventeen and pretty buff from working out. There were older women working there, and they all loved me.

One sunny afternoon, while sitting at my desk typing, I looked out the window and saw this girl walking down the street. I thought she was super fine, with huge hips and a booty, and I had to meet her. I dropped everything I was doing, ran outside, and caught up with her at the corner. I asked for her name, and she surprised me when she responded, "Darryl, you know who I am. I'm Brian's sister."

I knew her brother, Brian, and then remembered that I had actually met her before when I was twelve and she was ten. One of my good friend's sisters had introduced us, and I knew she liked me back then, but I wasn't interested at the time.

I looked at her again and said, "Are you that little girl I met some years ago?" She said, "Yes." I said, "Damn! You've grown up!"

I told her I thought I could get her a job and asked for her phone number. She went inside, applied, and left without giving me the number.

A week or so later, I was taking out the trash at my

house when I saw her coming down the alley. I said, "Hey, what's going on? What happened to you? You never gave me your number." She immediately reached into her purse and pulled out a slip of paper with her number on it. At first, I hesitated, thinking, *Is she just walking around with her number in her purse?*

I took it anyway, and later I realized the whole thing had been a setup—I was the reason she came that way.

A few days later, she got hired at the daycare, and I spent the next few weeks following her around everywhere, always asking if I could help her. One day, I caught her alone in the copy machine room and managed to steal a kiss. However, one of the ladies saw us, and they fired her immediately.

I worked at the daycare all summer, and by the time my senior year started, I didn't want to do anything but hang out with her, drink, and smoke weed with my friends.

That year, I hardly went to any classes, but I always made time to carry her books and walk her to class. I kept hanging out with her and my friends, drinking and getting high, even though she didn't drink or smoke. I was never a huge drinker, but I loved my weed.

Eventually, I failed three or four classes and had to choose between repeating my senior year or going to summer school. There was no way I was going back for another year, so I chose summer school. They sent me to a school across the river with all the white kids.

I was pretty popular over there and connected with some kids who I knew could get me some weed. I decided to focus on my classes since I had made no effort all school year. I ended up earning all A's that summer and graduated with my class of 1978, but I wasn't allowed to walk the stage. That bothered me for years. Though I was never proud of how I had earned my diploma, at least I had accomplished that much—I had it.

Now, I didn't want to go to college, but I had to get away from my dad. He wasn't happy with me bringing girls into the house or smoking weed, and we were on each other's last nerve. So, I enlisted in the Air Force. As I mentioned earlier, I had been deaf in my right ear since infancy. When I took the hearing test, I noticed the sound always came through my left (good) ear first, and I was sharp enough to pick up on that. But when it moved to my right ear, I tried timing the sequence and pressing the button accordingly.

Apparently, I flunked the first three hearing tests. On the fourth try, they put me in an isolated booth. As before, the sound started in my left ear, and when it switched to my right ear, I looked around—no one was watching. So, I turned the headphones around, passed the test, and got into the Air Force.

I had chosen the Air Force because I wanted to be around airplanes. But my sergeant in basic training looked just like Arthur Fonzarelli from *Happy Days*—except he was mean as hell. One day, I asked him, "When are we gonna see some planes?" He shot back, "Boy, you ain't never gonna see no goddamn airplanes."

That's when I lost all my motivation. It was scorching hot in San Antonio that summer—averaging 115 degrees. I remember reading in the newspaper that violent crimes were down because if someone was angry enough to hurt you, they'd drive you out of town, make you take off your shoes and socks, and force you to walk back. People were showing up at the ER with second- and third-degree burns on their feet.

I was the fastest in my platoon and doing well in boot camp, but during my third week, my drill sergeant whispered something in my bad ear, and I couldn't hear him.

"Boy, did you hear what I said?" he asked.

"Yeah, I heard you, but say it again," I replied.

He repeated it, and, of course, I didn't hear a thing. He immediately sent me to the doctor, who ran several tests, confirmed I was deaf in one ear, and set me up for discharge.

I spent the next few weeks hanging out in the officers' club, eating great food, and playing basketball—until one day, I was called into the captain's office. He asked what had happened, and I told him the whole truth about how I had manipulated the hearing test just to get away from my dad. He shook his head and said he hoped I had learned a lesson. Then, he sent me home with an honorable medical discharge, a bald head, and two hundred dollars in my pocket.

I bummed around for a month or two. One day, while talking to my dad about how many girls I had, he cut me off.

"Boy, shut the hell up. You can't even buy a girl a damn hot dog."

That hit me hard because he was right. But it also lit a fire in me. I told myself that he would never be able to say that to me again.

Shortly after that conversation, I found out that my mom had a friend who worked for the State of Pennsylvania's testing department. My mom set up a meeting with her, and I went down to meet her. She was an older woman in her forties, recently divorced, with grown children. I was a handsome, well-mannered, buffed-up eighteen-year-old. She offered to tutor me at her house.

When I got there, I noticed she had candles lit, and it smelled really good. She asked if I wanted a glass of wine, and I said, "OK." We sat down and talked for a while, and then she told me that she was going to give me all the answers to the test. She asked me to sit in the back of the room and destroy the answers when I was done, which I did. I don't think I ever saw her again.

Since serving time in the Air Force, I had a ten-point veteran's preference going into the test, and my final grade was 109. That score made me the top candidate on the civil service list that year, and I had opportunities for several well-paying jobs.

I accepted a job coding death and birth certificates. It paid eighteen thousand dollars a year and had great benefits. I was still living with my parents, and within a month or two, I had a brand-new 1978 Chrysler LeBaron. You couldn't tell me anything—I was on top of the world, "Diggin' the scene with a gangster lean, gangster whitewalls," and thought I was the shit.

After working there for two years, I saw myself going nowhere, growing old, and still doing that job like the older ladies I worked with. I was the only male and the only Black employee. I decided it was time to go to college, and one week before I was going to put in my resignation, I got laid off. I went to college, collecting one hundred dollars every week in unemployment for my first year there.

I decided to study information technology, but my first year, all I did was get high and party. I ended up with a 1.8 GPA and was immediately put on academic probation. The next year, I straightened up and earned a 3.0. I was going into my senior year when I ran out of money and had to drop out.

When my girlfriend graduated, she enrolled in the same college, and we became a couple on campus. One day, I had to return home to sign up for my unemployment benefits. On the way back, it was winter—a beautiful sunny day— but a snow blizzard started. By the time we had only gotten a quarter of the way back to school, there was already over a foot of snow, and it was still pouring down. Cars were all over the road and in ditches.

I was driving her Ford Maverick, which didn't have snow tires, so I was driving slowly and carefully because I didn't want to slide and get stuck in a ditch. We had made it almost all the way back when the car started sliding to the left, then to the right, until it stopped in the middle of the highway, blocking both lanes. I tried moving forward and backward several times, but the car wouldn't budge.

Suddenly, we saw a tractor-trailer coming straight at us. It was about two hundred yards away. I frantically tried again to move the car, but it still wouldn't budge. She started screaming, "Let's jump out!" as the truck got closer. It didn't look like the truck was going to stop—if it did, it would have likely slid off the road, too. I said, "Let me try one more time," and just at that moment, I hit reverse. Somehow, the car snapped into the right lane just in time, and the truck sped past us, blaring its horn in the left lane.

I knew then that it was another miracle in my life and that God was with us. But my nerves were so bad that my whole body was shaking for the rest of the trip. We finally got back to school, parked the car, and as we were getting out, some white boys at the top of a hill started hollering "niggers" at us and throwing snowballs. I was already in a bad mood, so I ran up the hill after them. They all scattered into the dorm, and I went up and down the hallway, cursing and daring them to come out, but they never did.

Looking back on my school years and my work with kids today, I see the importance of a parent—or at the very least, a mentor—guiding and motivating a child. When given proper guidance and motivation, a child will work to make that parent or mentor proud and will continue to excel. Without proper guidance, a child is left to make decisions based on peer pressure, TV/videos, and the streets—which, in most cases, will be detrimental to their life.

The Bible tells us in Proverbs 22:6:
"Train up a child in the way he should go, And when he is old he will not depart from it."

TRIALS AND TRIBULATIONS

At the age of seventeen, I started dating my wife. I was wild and very immature, and she was a good girl. She didn't smoke, drink, or even hang out, and that's all I wanted to do.

Through the years, she put up with a lot of craziness that I put her through. I wanted my cake and eat it too, as they say. In 1982, I had my first child, a beautiful daughter from someone I hardly knew. I didn't believe she was mine and asked for a DNA test. It came back 99.89%, and I still didn't want to accept it.

After a few years had passed, I heard that my daughter, whom I had still never seen, was running around outside her grandmother's home. I asked my brother Billy if he would ride down there one day and look for her and come back and tell me what he thinks. After a week or so, I got together with Billy and asked him if he had gone down there. He responded, "Now you know I love you, bra, but that girl looks just like you."

So, I finally accepted that I had a daughter but was confronted with the situation of how I was going to keep this from my girlfriend. I began to get phone calls at my mother's house from an unknown caller threatening to tell my girl, or he would say that he was going to tell her and "fuck her." So, I had to break down and tell her before she found out through the streets. It took a while, but we eventually got through it. When the caller called the next time, I told the dude, "Yeah, motherfucker, she knows. Now what the fuck you got? Because if I ever find out who this is, I'm gonna fuck you up." He replied, "You ain't never gonna find out who this is, motherfucker," and hung up. That was the last call from him, and I never found out who it was.

My parents loved my girlfriend, and my mom taught her all of her recipes. My girlfriend started cooking for her family when she was twelve or so. Her mother had to go out to work, and she became the mother of their home. She had six brothers and a sister. She was a sweet and kind of shy girl, who was quiet around people she didn't really know, but always had a big heart for helping others. On the other hand, I was loud, boastful, and didn't give a damn. We were total opposites.

I got a job as a programmer I with the PA Department of Public Welfare. When I applied for the state job, I was actually short three college credits to qualify due to failing a required class that was graded on a Pass or Fail basis. Being the artist that I was, I changed an "F" to look like a "P" on my transcripts and got set up for the interview. While in college, there was a girl that I had made friends with, and she did all my labs and tests for me, so even though I had studied computers in college, I actually knew nothing about them.

It happened to be that there was a freeze on hiring at the state for about three months before my interview was scheduled, and I went to the library and got a lot of books on computer programming. I had the gift of gab, and I figured if I could at least talk like I knew a little, I could get the job. I studied those books for three months, and when the interview came, I nailed it and got the job. I worked there for a year, learned everything I could by studying other programs, and eventually got really good at it.

Shortly afterward, my girl and I got our own apartment, where we lived for a year. Then in 1983, she wanted to get married. I was not at all interested in getting married because I was still having fun with my friends and hanging out. She eventually gave me an ultimatum, and I didn't want to lose her, so I agreed but still was not into it.

We got married on her birthday in February 1984, and later that year, we purchased our first home. At twenty-four years old, I was married and had my own home. I was happy, working, and still hanging out as much as I could. After working there for a year, I was promoted to Programmer II with the PA State Police, where I was very instrumental in programming their fingerprinting system. After working two years there, I started working as a contractor for the Department of Defense, programming their parts weaponry system and had top security clearance.

In November 1986, we had our first son. It was an exceptionally warm and sunny day in Pennsylvania for that time of the year, and I was so excited and proud. I went to several Lamaze classes on childbirth. They showed videos of the baby slowly coming out, and in many cases, they had to use stirrups to help the baby to come out. That was not the way he came out; he squirted right out, and I was amazed. I remember bringing him home, and I picked him up and looked deep into his eyes and saw all the things I had done in my life that I was not proud of. I put him down and prayed that God would shield him from my trials and tribulations that I had gone through at that point in my life.

I was still running the streets, but I loved my wife and wanted to be a better man, husband, and father. We decided to go to church, and one Wednesday, we went to Bible study. The study was on King David and his servant Uriah. Uriah was one of his most loyal servants. He would even sleep on the steps of the castle, and David would tell him to go home.

One day, David saw his wife Bathsheba bathing and wanted her, so he organized a plot to have Uriah killed and then took his wife as his own. David, his kingdom, and his family went through chaos and suffered for three years. Finally, King David took off all his clothes and begged God for forgiveness. God had mercy on him, forgave him, and lifted the curse. This is, of course, the short version of the story. However, at the end of the study, we were told that the moral of the story was that we can sin, and God will forgive us, but there is a price we will have to pay.

I slipped away to the altar afterward and prayed for God to forgive me, and asked Him, "If there is a price I have to pay, please do it quickly and get it over with." The very next day was my dad's birthday, and my mother sent me out to the grocery store to get some items she had forgotten. At the end of the street, as I was making a left at the light, a hospital van came through and hit me head-on.

I found myself out of work on disability for eight months. During that time, some guys I knew introduced me to crack cocaine. I had no idea what I was getting myself into, as it was relatively new to the neighborhood, and before I knew it, I was hooked and running wilder than ever before. I spent three years running the street with this addiction, just as King David was cursed, and what I had actually prayed for.

During those three years, my life was chaotic. I was a functional addict. I never missed a day of work, and that was because I knew I had to work to get money for the drugs. I found myself in dark houses, basements, and motels smoking crack, going back and forth to the dealer, until all my money was gone, and I knew I had to go home. I would get paid on Friday and wouldn't come home until Sunday when my bank account was emptied. I sold everything of value, including jewelry, TVs, and even had my car repossessed. When my car was being repossessed, all I could think about was that I would have more money to smoke.

I don't even know how I had enough money for gas or lunch to go to work. I guess even though God was chastising me, He still continued to allow me to be functional because He was not done with me. When I would come home after being out for days, my wife would argue and fuss at me. My friends and family would try to talk to me, but it all went in one ear and out of the other. I didn't give a damn about anything they were saying. Girls who were addicted were the worst. They would do anything for another hit of cocaine, and I mean anything. I even heard stories of them having sex with dogs for another hit.

I did try to quit on several occasions. I went to several rehabilitation facilities and came out each time with my mind programmed that I was done with the drug, but my heart was still in love with those people, places, and things, and I would always go back within a few days or a week or two. My wife was very frustrated with me and couldn't understand how I could do this to my family. On payday, she would have to beat me to the ATM and withdraw all the money before I could get there and withdraw it for more drugs, so she would be unable to pay the bills. She felt betrayed, and though she prayed for me, she felt alone and abandoned.

I never did anything that was intended to hurt anyone or steal from anyone, but as I was approaching the third year of this addiction, I was talked into going out of town to Reading, PA, and robbing some Cuban guys out of their cocaine. I may have been addicted to the drug and have done things that I was not proud of, but I had never been a gangster. When we got there and the guy came out with the cocaine, my friend took the cocaine, and I had my hand in my jacket as if I had a gun, and he begged for his life. I didn't even have a knife, and we got away with two ounces of cocaine. I was gone several days before I came home.

On the way home, I remember falling asleep at a red light and then waking up to see cars passing me. I was fortunate that a policeman didn't come by. I finally arrived home to find my wife and son gone, and they had taken almost everything from the house. I cried about them being gone and for how terrible of a husband and father I'd been. But, I still had a quarter ounce of cocaine left, and though I found myself crying about my family, the drug was still talking to me.

Several of my family members and friends were knocking on the door, wanting to help me in any way they could. I wouldn't let anyone in, and even when my dad came, I told him, "Come back in the morning, and I'll be ready to go." I smoked all of that cocaine that night, and God only knows how I didn't overdose.

In the morning, my dad picked me up and took me to the hospital before taking me to another rehab. For the first time, I had to make a real decision. I had to decide if my family or the streets and drugs were more important to me. This was the point when my programmed mind came into sync with my heart, and I chose my family. It was a thirty-day rehab, and I called my dad in fourteen days and told him I was done and to come and get me. I had lost my job, my car, jewelry, and everything that was of value to me. My wife found it in her heart to come back home, and I began trying to move forward in my life.

The first several weeks, I would wake up in severe sweats—so much that my body was drenched like I had gotten out of a swimming pool. My wife said that Satan had his hands on me. Then, one night, I had a dream that I was walking with Christ. We never spoke, but my spirit told me who He was. I was so overjoyed, excited, and overwhelmed by His presence. Just to be walking with Him, I felt glorified. Then suddenly, He turned and began to fade as He was backing away, and I screamed, "No, don't leave me, take me with you." He replied, "No, you can't come with me now, my son." I woke up crying profusely, and I never had another sweat.

I know had He taken me, I wouldn't be here today. I learned that God speaks to us through the Holy Spirit in our unconscious minds, in dreams, through our spirit and conscience, and through other people. He did it in the Bible, and He still does it today, so I know that was a real visit that evening in my dream. God gave me what I asked for in my prayer, but in a manner that I would have never expected and for the same three years as in the scriptures. What resonates in my soul from this experience, even today, is that He said that, "I couldn't come now." The word "now" gives me hope and faith that one day I will be there with Him, giving Him all the honor, glory, and praise.

Looking back, one thing that I learned is this: During the three years of my addiction, others would talk to me about what I was doing, and I can remember telling them that I didn't understand why they were so concerned, because I was only affecting myself. The truth in this reality is that everything we do, be it positive or negative, affects everyone that loves us. Life was not all about me, but also about all those around me who loved me as I loved them. That meant leaving all of those negative people, places, and things behind and searching for the positive people, places, and things in my life.

After that, I got a better job than I ever had within days and got back everything that I had lost, including the respect of my wife, family, and friends. I learned that God is not a taker, though He will allow Satan to test you and take from you. He is a giver, and whatever He allows Satan to take from you, once you've learned your lesson and come through the trial or tribulation, He will give you back more than was taken from you, and I am a witness to that today. We see this also illustrated in the life of Job.

Soon afterwards, He blessed me with another son in September 1991, and I couldn't have been any happier in my life at that time. He was a week or two late, and my wife and I had gone to Burger King just before a checkup that was scheduled. We met the doctor at the hospital, and after examining her, the nurses and doctor went into emergency mode. Suddenly, they had me in a gown and took us to a surgical room. I was in panic mode and asked, "What is going on?" I was told the child was not showing expected movements, and they were about to do an immediate c-section.

I was in shock as I sat there on the other side of the curtain that was covering her, and the only thing I could see was her feet. As I sat there and they began the procedure, I could hear squishing noises and smell blood as they were removing him. After they got him out and we saw that he was okay, I decided to peek over the curtain and see what they had done. It was the worst thing I had ever seen. It looked like she had been cut in half, and I got weak and nauseous and fell back into the seat. I got myself together and held my gorgeous son for the first time.

Shortly after he was born, we moved into a suburban part of town, bought a beautiful single-family home that God allowed us to fix up immaculately. I was making more money than ever before, and I was on top of the world. That is, until my mother passed in 1997.

After my mother passed, I was devastated. I didn't care about anyone or anything anymore. I stayed in my basement for weeks crying and watching old videos of my mother during various holidays and events. I quit my job, started running the streets again, and actually wanted to kill myself. Then, on the following New Year's of my mother's passing, my dad went down south to spend the holiday with my brother and sister, who were living in the Atlanta area at the time.

He locked the house, and I wasn't able to get in. I desperately wanted to get in so that I could feel the presence of my mother somehow. That night, on New Year's Eve, I was so depressed that I relapsed, spent the evening smoking crack, and didn't come home until early in the morning.

My wife and I were headed very quickly toward a divorce, and I knew it. Then, like always, God stepped in to help and guide me again. The next day, I found myself in between sleep and awake, and a voice spoke to me. It was as clear as if someone were right in the room talking to me, and it said these words: "Go down south, and you will look back on your life and say it was the best thing you have ever done." There was no dream, no conversation, just the voice telling me to go south.

When I awoke, I was compelled to leave. It was as though someone else was controlling me. As my wife was leaving to go to work, I told her I was leaving. She didn't believe me and never even looked back at me as she was walking out of the house.

I had two cars at the time, and I packed my primary vehicle with all my clothes and things I thought were necessary, and I packed my other car with everything else. I called one of my friends to come get the other car and made him promise that he would drive my car with all my belongings in it once I was ready for them.

I drove to Chattanooga, TN, where my sister was living, with fifty dollars in my pocket. I made my family promise not to tell anyone, including my wife (especially), where I was. I got there and put my resume out on the internet and received lots of calls. At one point, we couldn't answer the phone fast enough between calls. My intention was to go to Atlanta to be close to my brother Tommy, and I did get a good offer in Atlanta, but then I got an offer to work in Nashville, TN.

At first, I wasn't at all interested because I am not a fan of country music, but the recruiter assured me that Nashville offered a lot more than just country music. He offered for me to come, allow him to take me to lunch, and show me around. I accepted, and my sister and I drove down. It was about an hour and a half away from her home in Chattanooga. I was very impressed with the city, and the pay was phenomenal. It came with a twenty-five-hundred-dollar signing bonus and a really nice three-bedroom condo overlooking the pool for three months.

I called my friend and asked him to bring my things; he agreed and left the next day. I had a week or so before I started the new job, and I called my wife. I told her where I was, about my new job, and asked her to pack up the house and move to TN with me. By the grace of God, she agreed, and the following week, I went home and drove my family back. And I have said from the first day that "it was the best thing I've ever done."

Again, I saw God's presence in my life. He has always been with me since I was born and as a little kid when I fell in love with His son. I realize that sometimes God has to take you through some very dramatic situations to get you to the place He wants you. He will also put people in certain places at certain times to help and guide you to where He wants you to be. He put my wife in that place for me when I was twelve years old and first was introduced to her. Had it not been for her love, devotion, and patience in my life, I don't believe I would have made it, and I thank God for her.

Going through our trials and tribulations creates testimonies that can be very painful experiences. It serves to bring us closer to Him and make us better human beings, better husbands, wives, brothers, sisters, and even better friends. It guides us to submit our lives to Him and motivates us to give Him all the praise, honor, and glory. Those testimonies define our lives, make us stronger and wiser, so that they become a shield of honor and courage, which allows us to help others going through similar situations.

During the bright times in our lives, when the sun is shining on us, we feel that God is with us and that we are in communication with Him. However, during those dark days of life, when bad things happen, or everything seems to go wrong, we feel that God is not with us, that He is not listening to our prayers. Know that He is always with us, but I've learned that He will either test us or chastise us.

A test is intended to teach us, and when it's over, we will come out stronger and wiser. A chastisement is for us to realize our wrongs and make a change. Both can be painful, but a chastisement can even lead to death if a change is not made.

I consider the three years of my addiction a chastisement. I truly believe that if I had not made a change, I would not be alive today, but God judges us from our heart, and He had other plans for me. After moving south, we have never looked back, and God has never left us or forsaken us. But He wasn't quite done with me yet.

II

A NEW BEGINNING

TEST OF FAITH

After we moved to Nashville, TN, things were going great. We stayed in the apartment for two months and were able to buy a brand-new, beautiful home. It was the largest and nicest home we had ever had. We put a deck on the back that had two levels, and we had some good times on that deck grilling, partying, and playing dominoes.

I was referred to a guy who, I was told, could get me plugged into what was going on in Nashville. I called him and got his answering service. To make an impression, I told him that I was "DA from the PA" and had some questions for him. He called back, and we immediately became friends. Through him, I made a lot of friends and became a member of a black network that promoted business and social interaction.

I was working and having a great time building my network and partying with my new professional friends. We had great cookouts on our deck, and the fellas and I would drink and play dominoes until the wee hours of the morning. This went on for years, and I thought it would never end. I was making a lot of money, and we were living large.

My wife was getting acclimated to her new environment, and the kids were making lots of new friends in their new schools. For almost a year, my wife didn't work. She was getting bored and got a job with an insurance company, making decent money. It began to feel like home again, and we were really settling in.

The contract I was working on decided to outsource their Information Technology division to IBM. They brought in all of their own people and dropped the contract with the consulting firms that were working for them.

I was quickly able to land a contract at a local shoe manufacturing company that paid really well, and things seemed to be still working out. It was an 18-month contract, but we got so much done in six months that they laid most of us off. I struggled to find another contract after that and finally got another one, but it was in Knoxville, TN, which was two and a half hours away. I decided to take the job, get a little apartment there, and come home on the weekends.

I borrowed one of my friend's trucks, moved some furniture and things I needed, and settled into the apartment. I drove home every weekend and hated every minute of being away from my family. They came up and spent a weekend with me. We went to Dollywood, and I took the boys on a helicopter ride. But when they left, I was pretty depressed, though I had to try and make the best of it.

After a few months on that contract, it ended, and I found myself packing up and moving back home. I wanted to go home and be with my family anyway, but after that, I found myself out of work for a year or so. I was too qualified to work at Walmart and couldn't find another job in my field. I did what I could to make ends meet, but the mortgage was getting seriously behind.

To get grocery money, I once put out flyers for leaf cleaning and got a call. I went out and quoted the job at

$300. I took the whole family out to help. I thought it would be good to show my boys that a man does whatever he has to in order to provide for his family without selling drugs. After working a few hours, I realized that I had way underbid the job. We worked our butts off all day for that $300, but we needed it, and we got the groceries we needed with it.

We had been attending a large Baptist church for years, though we never joined because there were thousands of members, and even though we liked the message the pastor gave, it was way too large for what we were really looking for in a place to become members. We were tithing and were told that the church had been known to help people. I sent them an email explaining our situation and never heard back from them.

The mortgage company was now threatening to start foreclosure proceedings, and I needed to make drastic moves. I had no idea what to do, but one night I woke up in the middle of the night and had a solution. I would modify my resume to reflect sales. I had the gift of being able to talk to people, and I had read that the mortgage industry was doing well. I didn't know much about the mortgage industry, but I had purchased several homes over the years, and I understood about interest rates.

I left most of my previous jobs in good standing and still had contacts with several of my previous managers. I called each one of them up, explained my situation, and asked them to give me a reference related to sales if they received a call, and they all agreed. I applied to a local mortgage brokerage company and got hired. Our situation was serious because our credit was bad, we had no money, and if something didn't turn around for us, we could have found ourselves homeless.

The job required making cold calls to prospective customers and setting up appointments to go to their homes and structure deals for home purchases or to refinance their current mortgages and give them cash out to pay off bills or whatever the need was. It was a 100% commission job, and I was great at it. I was the top loan officer out of over twenty loan officers in the office on most months. But working 100% commission meant that my income was like a roller coaster. One month I'd make a killing, but with the mortgage so far behind, most of the money all went to catching it up. Then the next month or two might not be so good, and the mortgage fell behind a month or two again.

I got another mortgage position that came with a good base salary plus commission, and it was an opportunity to make pretty good money again, but we were so far behind on the mortgage, we knew that we were about to lose the home. My wife and I began praying, getting up from our prayers crying. After weeks of this, my spirit told me to stop praying or start having faith in my prayers and stop crying. I conveyed that to my wife, and we decided that was what we were going to do.

Having true faith meant that we had to get up from our prayers like we already had what we were looking for. My wife still did not want to leave the home but realized it was inevitable, and we started praying with faith for God to give us a new home. We got up from our prayers like we already had one, and the next day, we decided to go and find one, even though we didn't have much money.

We drove about a mile or so from the house and saw a house that had a "for-rent" sign on it. I called the owner, and a very sweet lady showed up. We talked, and I was able to negotiate a two-year rent-to-own deal. The only money she required down was the first month's rent of $700. We couldn't believe it, so we put the deposit together and got the key.

The house did require a lot of work to get it to our standard of living. I remember some of our family and friends stopping by to see the house and having very empathetic looks on their faces, as though we had fallen from grace. But we knew that God had us covered and were walking in 100% faith. We worked on the house for three months before we moved in.

I was doing great at my new job, and before long, we had that house looking like new money. It was the nicest home on the block. We learned the true value of faith during this test in our lives, and we never looked back. God continued to bless us with prosperity, and we stayed in the home for fifteen years. We built a huge screened-in deck on the back, and I found myself with friends there every day.

Even though God had been showing me His love, devotion, and power in my life for all these years, I still was not ready to submit my life to Him and change from some of my bad habits. Like many people do, when times were hard, I prayed, and God would bring me through my tribulation. But as soon as I got on the other side, the prayers and communication with Him stopped. Though my prayers may have stopped or become far and few between, His love and direction for my life never did.

In 2007, I started working in a sales position selling fuel cards to trucking companies. The job started off with a good salary plus commission, but as commission was supposed to rise, the salary decreased. During this time, the economy was in a recession, companies weren't spending, and I wasn't making any sales or commission. I became very depressed and didn't go to work for a whole week. I laid around, feeling evil thoughts of suicide and all sorts of crazy things. One day, my spirit told me to get up and go to work. On the way to work, I decided to stop and get some breakfast. I didn't care if I was late getting there or not.

While standing in line waiting to order and looking up at the menu, I felt a man standing behind me, and it felt as though he was looking at me. I turned and asked him, "What's up?" He responded and began telling me that he was homeless. I said to him, "I'm so sorry to hear that," but he quickly responded that he had everything he needed and not to feel sorry for him. He was living under a church pavilion, had a radio, blanket, pillows, and that God was taking care of him and giving him everything that he needed. I turned, and as I looked back at the menu, my mind started racing, thinking that I had a family, home, cars, food in the refrigerator, and this man had nothing, but was satisfied and giving God the glory. I turned back to buy him breakfast, and to my amazement, he was gone. I ran to the door to try and catch him, and he was blocks down the street.

I ate my breakfast and went to work. When I got there, I told my manager that I couldn't work there another day, and I quit. It was the first time I had ever quit a job without having another one lined up. I had no idea what I was going to do, but it was as though ten pounds had been lifted off of my shoulders. The next day, I got a call for an interview for a sales position with a communication company making fifty thousand dollars annually, plus commission. I was surprised because I had never applied for this position.

I went on the interview and told a joke to the panel of five people, and they all fell out laughing. On my way home, the recruiter called me and told me that I had the job. I asked him where he got my information from, and he replied that he had found my resume on the internet. I thought it was very strange because that resume had been on the internet for years. That's when I realized that this was another blessing or intercession from God, and that He put that man at that very spot to tell me his story. He already had this job set up for me. By His grace, I did very well in the position and stayed for several years.

As time passed after I got this job, I never lost my spirit and my love for Christ, but I was not in communication with Him. At one point, I decided that I didn't even want to be a Christian anymore. I was tired of the pimping pastors and the hypocritical members. The church that we had been going to was across the street from a Kroger grocery store, and after church would let out, many of the members would come there and shop, and wouldn't even speak to you. I said that I was done with Christianity.

I wanted to get back to my communication and relationship with God, though, and so we started visiting an Islamic mosque. We didn't feel any love in there, and after studying the Quran for a while, I wasn't willing to believe in Christ as a prophet and not the Son of God. I was really struggling with this until one day, I was going along, and it felt as though someone had tapped me on the shoulder.

I turned around, and it was like a walk on the Damascus Road. I saw a bright light, and I could hear Christ say to me, "Look at all the times I've carried you through your trials and tribulations." Instantly, it was like I was watching a movie of all the times that Christ had carried me through all of my trials and tribulations. My jaw dropped, and I stood there watching this for I don't know how long.

When it ended, I knew that Islam was not for me, and I had to find my way back to my prayers and back to church. It was time to truly submit my life to Christ, to be born again, and become a new man.

Born Again

After my walk on the Damascus Road, my wife and I started visiting churches but couldn't really find one we felt the spirit we were looking for. We had been invited to a church by one of my friends who sang there, but we could never find it. Then one day, as we were riding down an adjacent street to it, there it was like a shining star.

We said we would go there next Sunday. The first day

we went there, I felt my spirit tell me that this was where I needed to be, and I joined the second time I went back. I loved the pastor and the congregation and became very active in the church, doing all I could to serve Christ. Soon afterwards, they made me a deacon.

In 2013, I was contacted by a man in South Carolina who had heard about my sales accomplishments and offered me an opportunity to build teams for him selling Dish Network. I went, met with him, and he told me that he was going to make me rich. It was the first time a rich person had ever said they had plans to make me rich, and I accepted the offer.

For the next three months, I worked in South Carolina, deep parts of Georgia, and Mississippi selling Dish Network products and services. I found myself in some very poor neighborhoods. I never knew people were really that poor in today's world. Some of them lived in old wooden shacks that resembled several hundred-year-old slave quarters.

Dish Network required a credit card and good credit. Many of the neighborhoods I was in were poor people who didn't have a credit card. I never received the resources that I needed to build the teams we had discussed, and the deal he made with me never really materialized. After three months of sleeping in motels and being away from home, I decided to quit.

When I returned home, I began to develop rashes on my sides. I went to the dermatologist, and after several skin tests, they were unable to tell me what was causing the rashes. They started giving me steroid shots and ointments that I would apply. The shots and ointments would work for a few weeks, but the rashes continued to return. This went on for three years.

Toward the end of the third year, I stopped taking the steroid shots and just used the ointment. I developed a rash that wouldn't go away, regardless of how much ointment I applied. I began praying for weeks, asking God to remove this rash, but nothing was happening. I felt He wasn't listening to my prayers and couldn't figure out what I had done to cause this curse to come upon me. Then, I became very depressed.

One day, my pastor called me to the church to watch over things while he had to attend a meeting and had guys working on some wiring in the church. I went, and after the pastor returned, I explained to him that I was depressed and told him about the rashes I'd been having for three years, as well as the one I currently had. We went into his office, prayed, and he took me to 2 Corinthians 12:6-10:

"Therefore, in order to keep me from becoming conceited, I was given a thorn in my flesh, a messenger of Satan, to torment me. Three times I pleaded with the Lord to take it away from me. But he said to me, 'My grace is sufficient for you, for my power is made perfect in weakness.' Therefore, I will boast all the more gladly about my weaknesses, so that Christ's power may rest on me. That is why, for Christ's sake, I delight in weaknesses, in insults, in hardships, in persecutions, in difficulties. For when I am weak, then I am strong."

Afterwards, for the first time, I gave up on doctors and

steroids. I submitted to God's will and said to Him, "Lord, Your grace is sufficient for me, and if this rash never goes away, I will delight in my weakness so that Your power may resonate in my life and in my testimony to others." After this, within twenty-four hours, the rash went away, and I have never had another one in the many years since.

This testimony made me understand the true power of God's ability to heal through faith and belief in His promises. Prior to this, I didn't believe in healing. I'd seen so many fake healings in the churches and on TV that I was turned off by any pastors or churches claiming to heal people. But after this experience, God showed me that He not only has the power to heal your body but also to heal and fix any situations you may be going through.

After this, I wanted to learn more about the Bible. I was amazed at how God worked in three-year increments in my life's trials and tribulations. My pastor advised that I go to a local seminary school that he had graduated from. I decided to try it, and in 2015, I took my first class. I fell in love with the school and all of the other brothers and sisters in Christ who were pursuing the same thing I was. Many of them were pastors or working toward becoming pastors, and others were there equipping themselves with the knowledge of the Bible so that they could be better servants of Christ and one day do some good and save souls.

My wife even got very involved with service work and did many things for the church, including cooking for special events. They gave her an opportunity to use her spiritual gift of interior decorating and making many decorations for the church. I learned that the number three in the Bible represents completeness, perfection, and divine wholeness. I then realized that each time God took me through a three-year trial, it was for me to enter the completeness of His grace and experience the complete and whole change in my life.

In 2017, the home values in the neighborhood we lived in doubled in value, and I thought it was time to sell and move. I believed the neighborhood was about to undergo a transformation, and values would go back down. I prayed about it, and like before, I had faith that God was going to work all things out for our good.

I had my credit scores looking pretty good and knew I had to qualify without using my wife, as her scores weren't very good at the time. I applied and was accepted immediately. We put our home on the market and began looking for a new one. We had done so much work on our home that I wanted a brand-new, ready-to-move-in home that didn't require any work.

We began looking and were having a hard time finding the right home. We had large furniture, and we needed a home that could accommodate a formal living room, dining room, family room, and a king-sized bed. As we searched, it seemed the new homes were always missing one of the rooms we needed for all of our furniture.

Our home sold in three days, and we had to decide on a home quickly. We found a home built in 2004. It was a huge, custom-made home, with way more space than we needed, but it did need some cosmetic work done badly. We decided to go for it, and in January 2017, we moved into what felt like a mansion to us. It was another gift from God for being committed servants and having faith. He gave us a larger and more beautiful home than we could have dreamed of.

I received my associate's degree in Christian education in 2018. This was a major accomplishment in my life due to the fact that I had never worn a cap and gown or walked a stage to receive a diploma or degree before. My family was so proud of me. My wife and I began reading the Bible together every night, and I would answer any questions she had.

In 2018, with the help of my cousin, I received a full scholarship, and in 2019, I received my bachelor's degree in biblical studies with a 4.0 GPA, only 12 credits away from my master's degree. I began doing some Bible studies and speaking on other occasions at the church.

I was interested in working in a ministry for youth, couples, and men. I felt it was something the communities desperately needed, and with all of my testimonies, I believed I could be a real asset in these areas. The church we were attending didn't have the ministries I was looking for and didn't seem very interested in starting one, so we began searching for another church closer to the home we were living in.

I had many pastor friends, and we visited several churches. One in particular, we really liked, and it had everything we were looking for, but it was forty-five minutes away from our home. Finally, we found a church that was five minutes from our home and offered everything we were looking for.

We joined the church, but before we could get grounded in the fellowship, there was a pandemic named COVID-19 that ravaged the entire world. In the United States, there were 1,209,009 confirmed deaths, the most of any country. The country basically had to shut down. People were warned to stay home and practice social distancing. Social distancing required people to stay at least six feet apart from one another and to wear gloves to prevent touching surfaces, as well as masks to prevent the spread of the virus from one person to another.

During this time, all nonessential businesses were ordered to shut down, along with all schools. The schools finally decided to close for the remainder of the year, and in many cases, graduations such as mine were put on hold or canceled altogether. After a few weeks, as the number of infected people and deaths began to level out, states decided to open some stores and start to get things back to normal, even though the experts were strongly against this reopening. However, the pandemic was getting worse, and people were getting sick and dying in record-setting numbers.

I was scheduled to graduate with my Doctorate in Theology, and since we were all social distancing and they were limiting gatherings of people to ten to fifty, on July 31, 2020, I graduated with a 4.1 GPA. God had brought me to a point in life where He gave me no excuse to quit, take a break, or slow down. He provided me with a scholarship that covered the last three years of my schooling.

Today, I can look back on my life and see Christ carrying

me during all of my trials and tribulations. He has always been there with me since the first day, and I am confident that He will never leave me. There were so many directions my life could have taken, but God had a plan for me that I had no idea of.

I had a dream where God took me to the year 1973, when I was thirteen years old. I was amazed at how easygoing life was then, with not many cars on the street, fewer people, and practically no violence. As I stood there in amazement, I asked God if I could go back and tell myself about the trials and tribulations I would go through in an effort to avoid them.

God then took me to Job 14:1-2: "Man who is born of woman is of a few days and full of trouble. He comes forth like a flower and fades away; he flees like a shadow and does not continue." He told me that "even if I escaped the trials and tribulations I had gone through, there would have been others."

Then I asked Him if I could go back and tell my brothers and sisters, and He took me to the story of the rich man and Lazarus in Luke 16:31: "He said to him, 'If they do not listen to Moses and the Prophets, they will not be convinced even if someone rises from the dead,'" and He told me that "my testimony would do them no benefit."

I made one last request and asked if I could go back to my senior year in high school. I believed I could have played football, run track, gotten a scholarship, gone to the Olympics, and played professional football. He said, "Yes, you could have, but you wouldn't have your family...

Is that what you want?" I replied, "No," and then I realized that there is nothing that I would or could have changed. Everything that has happened in my life has grown me into the man that God intended for me to become.

I thank God every day for allowing me the strength to endure and for pulling me out of my situations victorious. In Jeremiah 29:11, God tells us, "For I know the plans I have for you," declares the Lord, "plans to prosper you and not to harm you, plans to give you hope and a future." This verse has certainly been true in my life, and I know it can work in your life as well.

All we have to do is accept Christ as the Son of God, believe that He lived, taught, performed miracles, and died on Calvary for the sins of the world. Know that God does not look at you for who you are and what you may be doing now, but He looks at who you will become and what you will do for His kingdom.

The choice is yours. You can deposit all your valuables in the world of flesh and blood that lasts only a few days, or you can make your deposits in the spirit that will last eternally. I choose Christ and the Spirit because, as it says in Joshua 24:14-15: "Now therefore, fear the Lord, serve Him in sincerity and in truth, and put away the gods which your fathers served on the other side of the river and in Egypt. Serve the Lord! And if it seems evil to you to serve the Lord, choose for yourselves this day whom you will serve, whether the gods which your fathers served that were on the other side of the river, or the gods of the Amorites, in whose land you dwell. But as for me and my house, we will serve the Lord."

CONCLUSION

In Hebrews 13:5, God has said, "Never will I leave you; never will I forsake you." And in Jeremiah 29:11, He says, "For I know the plans I have for you," declares the Lord, "plans to prosper you and not to harm you, plans to give you hope and a future."

My life has been a testimony that He has never left or forsaken me, and that He had plans for me to prosper and have a future. Since birth, Satan tried to kill me, but God didn't allow it. He allowed him to take one of my ears, but God made my other ear twice as strong.

For years, He allowed Satan to fill me with lust, drugs, and alcohol. It corroded my mind, and though my mother filled me with love, it hindered my ability to truly love those who loved me. As a result, I almost lost everything and everyone that ever mattered to me. But God pulled me from the chaos and spoke to me on several occasions so that there would be no doubt that it was Him who was there for me. He turned my life around and gave me more than I could have ever imagined.

Today, I live in South Carolina with my beautiful wife of forty-one years, who has been by my side through it all. She has been my helper and my motivation, always believing in me and expecting the best from me. She is my best friend, and together, I believe we can accomplish anything.

It's been thirty-six years since I've been addicted to any drugs, and I walk humbly in my steps, giving God all the glory, all the praise, and all the honor for everything I have and everything I am. Without Him, I know I would be nothing, and most likely even dead by now. Today, I can fear no man, and with His strength and help, I have faith that I can handle any trial or tribulation that may come my way. I know He holds me in the palm of His hands and that He will never let go of me, and I will never let go of Him.

I live today to serve Him by using my knowledge and testimonies to help others avoid going through the same things I had to endure or to give them the courage to come out of the situation they may be in.

We live in a world of spiritual warfare, and Satan will always be out to kill, steal, and destroy. His primary goal is to set his will against the will of God, but the Bible teaches us that he has already lost the battle, and so we await the return of the true King, our Savior. Through Him, we have been saved by God's free gift of grace, by the shedding of His blood, and the sacrifice He made for us.

For God so loved the world that He gave His only begotten Son, that whomever believes in Him shall not perish but have everlasting life. 1 Thessalonians 4:16-17 teaches us that "For the Lord Himself will come down from heaven, with a loud command, with the voice of the archangel, and with the trumpet call of God, and the dead in Christ will rise first. After that, we who are still alive and are left will be caught up together with them in the clouds to meet the Lord in the air. And so, we will be with the

Lord forever."

Today, I live for the glorious day when I am face to face with our Lord, as I was in my dream so many years ago. I will never forget the wonderful feeling I had just walking with Him. There have been times when I wished He would have taken me then, but as He left my mother here for me when I needed her most, I was left here for my family and to make a difference in this world. One day, when we are face to face, I hope to hear Him say to me, "Well done, good and faithful servant! You have been faithful with a few things; I will put you in charge of many things. Come and share your master's happiness!"

To God be the power and the glory forever and ever!